Under the Covers

Whitney Ellison

BookLeaf
Publishing

India | USA | UK

Presentation by *BookLeaf Publishing*

Web: www.bookleafpub.com

E-mail: info@bookleafpub.com

ISBN: 9789357214612

First edition 2023

Wintering Haikus

1.
Hummingbirds moved south
Golden rays a darker shade
First frost come and gone

2.
Sleeping sunflowers
As great mystery takes hold
Ever changing shifts

3.
Energy cannot
Be created nor destroyed
Hot changes to cold

4.
So I'll bundle up
With my boots and a jacket
My lungs feel alive

5.
Trusting in design
Of the ultimate divine
Embracing winter

Staying the Course

When I am feeling restless
in a moment of stillness
Or a season of stillness
And the urge to control
the urge to make things happen
the urge to take matters
into my own hands again
The urge. The Urge.
THE URGE
becomes so strong that
my impulses vibrate
from my shoulders
down my wrists
out of my hands
Or quakes from my shoulders
up my neck
And out of my mouth;
I remind myself:
I am right where I'm supposed to be.

Remember, I say to Me,
the universe is curious:
am I still in a place of patience?
of receiving?
of allowing the unfolding?

Or

Am I going to invite the same
lesson in for another spar I will not win
And hold onto the pattern that
is not in service of my true desires?

Once I spell it out to Me
from a lens of patience,
respect and recognition,
the dragon of my impulses
goes back into her cave
And takes another nap
hoping her dreams
will be realized
in her slumber.

And they always are.

Under the Covers

Under the covers
The day shining bright
I wake from my slumber
Still missing the night.

Sleepy, my pillow
Becomes my new shade
As I roll over
My bed, still not made.

Blankets I pull
Tightly over my head
Pup stuffed down deep
In the cave of my bed.

Snuggled warm at my belly
Curled into spoons
Lying still and dreamy
Wishing for the moon.

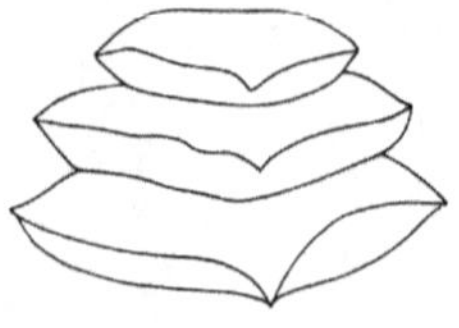

The Puzzle

I keep walking up to
this thousand piece puzzle
and painstakingly connecting little pieces.
It is not an easy puzzle,
these thousand pieces
that form a painted winter scene
with thick brush strokes,
lots of whites, yellows, oranges
reds, purples and browns
painted in broad, broad brush strokes
that all look the same
when jigsawed into a thousand little pieces.

I don't particularly enjoy this puzzle;
although I do enjoy the experience
of the soft snap of a puzzle piece
as it clicks into place, aligning just right.

The satisfaction of that click
is a true delight
and keeps me there to find another fit
and dopamine hit.

I think about how satisfying
it will be to finish this puzzle,
at least for a moment
when I snap in the last piece -
aligning on all sides,
the image becomes completely clear.
I will rest for a day or so,
admire my work
then break it down,
box it up,
and begin another.

Blue Song

Isn't it amazing how the blue contrasts
so perfectly pleasing to our eyes
among the reds and oranges and yellows and
how the breeze compliments the swinging
branches of leaves and
creates a visual symphony in which
the world receives the fallen ones ever so gently
as they dance to their finish
landing with a soft almost inaudible tap until a
foot finds them or a branch falls on them and
they give in with a satisfied crunch.

Soft

My jawline is
softer now
as is
my heart

I take a deep
breath
and then
fall apart.

Scattered, swirling
like leaves
from a
tree

I don't hold it
all in -
I let me
be me.

The Cooling

The pavement is
still warm
under my bare feet
but the days are
growing shorter.

The leaves are
still green
but no longer
as vibrant
or excited as
they were
at the cusp of June.

They are sleepy
and so am I
after a good run
with the sun.

But even the sun
is tired -
sleeping in now,
rising later and later.
So too is my body,
though I try to resist.

The seasons will
change, whether
I resist or not.

And that's fine,
because the fiery
oranges, reds
and hints of purple
from the sun
of the early mornings
do not disappear,
they just move into
the leaves, giving one
last performance
before turning to
an earthy brown,
falling off
the sleepy trees
and fading
back into the earth
until spring.

So too, will I fade
back into the
earthy brown
of a warm
knit sweater,
a comfortable pair

of sweats
or blue jeans,
thick socks, and laced boots that

separate my feet
from the cold pavement,
until the sun becomes
an early riser once more.

Cityscape

An imaginary
city skyline
made of
sky

Oranges, deep blues
reds and a
hint of purple

Late sunrises
predicting the colors
of the leaves
soon to come.

Love

I believe that when a person dies
their spirit rises
and bursts into
billions of tiny pieces—
Stardust some might say—
and it sprinkles the world
and the loved ones especially;
and even the ones who were
touched from afar
carry that continued
energy until they die
and then their spirits too
burst into stardust
coating their loved ones
and the ones they
touched from afar —
and that's how we carry each other
beyond the end of time.

Processing

My anger quickly
shifted to tears.
Much quicker this time.
And because my kids are home
I stepped into the shower and let them
blend with the hot water
rolling down my face,
into the drain.
Freely, I sobbed.

Then -
and here's how
I know I'm growing-
I laid down to nap
and sleep off the pain,
But instead, the child inside me
said, *Not this time.*
This time you are
going to honor your art,
critics be damned.

She grabbed my hand, as
I picked up my computer
and began moving words to page
until at last,
the tears dried and
I was able to keep moving forward
with my heart intact.

The Puppy Chase

I chased the puppy
through the house
much like I chase my toddler.
I almost could hear her screaming
NO Mommy!
as I ran circles
in frustration,
her little body
evading my hands
and my will
that I wanted so desperately
to force upon her.
These are my days right now.
A toddler and a puppy.
And who am I to complain?
One time not long ago,
these were the days of my dreams.

Algorithm

If I'm not in your
algorithm,
I trust that you'll find me
in divine timing —
or you won't —
and that will be divine too.

Napping

Taking a nap
affirms that the world
will go on without me
and be just fine.
I happily receive
this divine permission
to rest.

Rain and Shine

Give me the
Morning Breeze and
a rain that starts over my head
while I stare off in the distance
at a clear sky
where the Sun
rises and hopes
I am watching her.

She tells me,
Look! I will give you this gift
when you start your day with me.
I'm here, even in the rain.
Didn't you know?
Literal light
in the dark.

She paused.

But love the rain too
she said.
He gifted you with the
Breeze and the
peaceful sound
of a new day beginning.

Less

I want fewer passwords
and more
sun rises on my deck.
Less email
and more
coffee with friends.
No schedules
and morning walks with my little ones.
Less photo-worthy, stressful vacations
and more
weekend rest.
Less holding my phone,
and more
holding hands.
Less bluster
and more
poetry.

Ask Me Nothing

Ask me nothing.
I have no answers.
All I can know
is my own experience.
It's all you can know too.
Your experience.
Everything else is
but a projection.
Antidotal only to the
mouth from which it's released.

In re: Leaving Full Time Work

You know what's weird?

You can grieve something you don't necessarily miss.

Life is funny like that.

Witnessing

Witnessing the rain from a dry place
is like witnessing my thoughts
outside of my mind's eye.

There is something mystical and safe,
knowing it's natural and lovely to see,
while not actually being immersed in it.

Solstice (The Start of Winter in the North)

Step outside and
breathe deeply.
Witness the cold shock
filling your lungs.
How alive you are!
Watch the light return,
day by day, little by little,
breath by breath.

New Year

How about
not setting expectations
for the new year
other than

that the sun
continues to rise
each day

and that we continue to
Inhale
     and
Exhale
knowing that this is enough,

if only we see
each breath
each day
each year
as the miracle it truly is.